D0537031

101 Things I Learned® in Culinary School

101 Things I Learned® in Culinary School

Louis Eguaras with Matthew Frederick

illustrations by Matthew Frederick

Matthew Frederick is the series creator, editor, and illustrator.

Grand Central Publishing
Hachette Book Group
237 Park Avenue
New York, NY 10017
www.HachetteBookGroup.com

Printed in China

First Edition: May 2010
10 9 8 7 6 5

Grand Central Publishing is a division of Hachette Book Group, Inc. The Grand Central Publishing name and logo is a trademark of Hachette Book Group, Inc.

The Hachette Speakers Bureau provides a wide range of authors for speaking events. To find out more, go to www.hachettespeakersbureau.com or call (866) 376-6591.

The publisher is not responsible for websites (or their content) that are not owned by the publisher.

Library of Congress Cataloging-in-Publication Data
Eguaras, Louis.
    101 things I learned in culinary school / by Louis Eguaras with Matthew Frederick.—1st ed.
       p. cm.
    ISBN 978-0-446-55030-7
    1. Cookery—Study and teaching.   2. Cooks—Training of.   I. Frederick, Matthew.   II. Title.
III. Title: One hundred and one things I learned in culinary school.
    TX661.E58 2010
    641.5092—dc22
                                                                              2009037647

From Louis

To Agnes, for believing in me, for everything.

Author's Note

After more than twenty years teaching and working in the culinary arts, I am sure of one thing: a chef can never stop learning and growing. The culinary world is ever evolving, as familiar techniques and experiences continually give way to new ones and force chefs to reevaluate their comfort zones. A chef's understanding of food and cooking thereby needs to extend beyond knowledge of ingredients, technique, tools, and equipment. A chef must be a scholar of colors, textures, and fragrances. He or she must know the history of food, its chemistry and alchemy, the art of presentation, and how to keep customers safe. A chef has to know how to manage and meet customers' needs and expectations, how to create and manage budgets, and how to delegate and answer to those working around him or her.

If you aspire to work in the culinary arts, you may wonder if it is a career or a job. It is both. As a job, it demands strong organization, calm in the face of pressure, and an ability to plan ahead but adjust quickly. It requires working long hours on one's feet in crowded spaces, often in extreme heat and trying conditions. It asks that one remains focused on the task at hand while remaining aware of the orders, requests, and languages flying around. It can require monotonous hours of prep, such as peeling twenty or more pounds of potatoes at once, all of which will get used in a few hours of frenzied rush. If you see the culinary profession as a career and not merely a job, such challenges will be understood as steps toward mastery of the trade, and will further fuel your passion for the field.

This book aims to provide insight into many facets of the culinary world, from its business to its art. Lessons in terminology, cooking techniques, sanitation, presentation, and management are intended to be useful both in and out of the kitchen. So keep this book open on the kitchen counter or the coffee table, or put it in your tool box for easy access between classes. Slip it into your jacket pocket to read on the bus or to find solace after a busy day in the kitchen. Use it as a friendly reminder and refresher. But whatever you do—don't use it as a coaster!

Louis Eguaras, Chef Instructor

Acknowledgments

From Louis

Thanks to my mother, Maridel Gonzalez-Beckman; my stepfather, Kent M. Beckman; Ronald Ford; Walter Scheib; Patrice Olivon; Keith Luce; Mauro Daniel Rossi; Jeffrey Coker; Stephen Chavez; Mike Shane; Mike Malloy; Matthew Zboray; Bruce Whitmore; Glenn Ochi; Geraldine Reyes; Jayson McCarter; Paul Sherman; Robert Soriano; my chef instructor colleagues who appreciate the simple explanation of culinary techniques and terminology; my students for providing me a resource of what to present in this book; the United States Navy; and most importantly my beautiful wife and best friend, Agnes Castillo Jose-Eguaras.

From Matt

Thanks to Karen Andrews, David Blaisdell, Katharine David-Hays, Alex Fairbank, Sorche Fairbank, Tracy Martin, Camille O'Garro, Janet Reid, Kallie Shimek, Flag Tonuzi, Julie Usher, Tom Whatley, and Rick Wolff.

101 Things I Learned in Culinary School

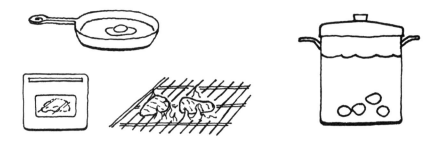

Dry cooking   Moist cooking

There are only two ways to cook.

Dry cooking uses direct heat—radiation, convection, or oil. Methods include sautéing, panfrying, deep-frying, grilling, broiling, roasting, and baking. It produces browning or searing of the food's outside surface.

Moist cooking uses water, stock, or other liquid (other than oil) as a medium for transferring heat. Methods include blanching, boiling, simmering, poaching, and steaming. The foods are not browned and tend to be tender when done. For best heat transfer, the cooking vessel should be large enough for the food to be completely surrounded by the liquid or steam.

Dry and moist methods can be combined. In braising and stewing, a tougher cut of meat is seared with dry heat, and then simmered for several hours in liquid to tenderize.

Paring knife: 2" to 4" blade, used to cut fruits and vegetables.

Boning knife: used to remove meat from a carcass. 5" to 7" firm blade.

Filet knife: 5" to 8" long pliable blade, used for filleting fish.

French (chef's) knife: versatile knife used for chopping, slicing, dicing, and mincing. 8" to 14" blade.

Serrated slicer: jagged, toothed blade, 12" to 14" long, used to cut bread and tomatoes.

Five knives do 95 percent of the work.

The well-equipped professional kitchen has a knife for every purpose, although the majority of cutting and chopping can be performed with a few knives. In general, it's better to buy fewer, higher quality knives as they will do more work with less effort, and are less likely to slip and break.

Most knife blades are stamped or forged. **Stamped knives** are made by using a template to cut a flat piece of metal. **Forged knives** are handcrafted with extreme heat that tempers the steel. Stamped knives are lighter and less expensive, but lack the overall quality and balance of forged knives and don't maintain sharpness as well. Blades may be made of:

Carbon steel: a mixture of carbon and iron. Often used for chef's knives because it is easy to sharpen, although it is readily discolored by acidic foods.

Stainless steel: the most common material in kitchens. It does not corrode or discolor and can last longer than carbon steel, but does not hold as sharp an edge.

High-carbon stainless steel: a mixture of carbon and stainless steel. Preferred by many chefs because it does not corrode or discolor, and is easy to sharpen.

Ceramic: neither stamped nor forged, but molded and fired from powdered zirconium oxide, a material second in hardness only to diamonds. Extremely sharp, rustproof, easy to maintain and clean, and nonreactive to acids.

Cookware: measured
across the top

Bakeware: measured across
the bottom

Don't buy a matched set.

No single cookware material is ideal for every use. Lighter pans are usually preferred for sautéing (it's easier to flip food), and heavier pans for searing (because they stay at the ideal temperature when cold food is added). Common materials are:

Stainless steel: lightweight, inexpensive, and nonreactive to acids. Not a good conductor; a layer of aluminum is usually included in the pot base to promote more even heat transfer.

Aluminum: lightweight, inexpensive, and a good heat conductor, but reactive to acids and easily dented. Anodized aluminum is less reactive and more durable.

Cast iron: heavy and durable. Heats evenly and maintains very high temperatures, making it ideal for browning/searing. Reactive to acids, thereby calling for regular seasoning (a protective layer of fat and carbon) to prevent rust. Enameled cast iron has a protective porcelain surface, eliminating the need for seasoning.

Carbon steel: durable, heats quickly, and like cast iron, requires regular seasoning. Good for woks, paella pans, and crepe pans.

Copper: has the best conductivity and most even heating, and responds quickly to temperature changes. Popular for sauces and sautéing. Expensive, reactive to acids, requires regular polishing.

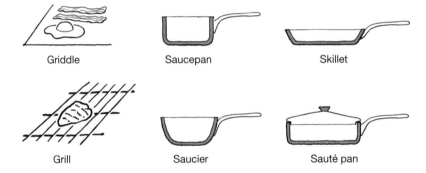

Griddle

Saucepan

Skillet

Grill

Saucier

Sauté pan

A griddle is not a grill, a saucepan is not a saucier, and a skillet is not a sauté pan.

A **griddle** is a piece of heavy cooking equipment with a continuous flat surface. A **grill** is an open web on which foods are placed to directly expose them to fire.

Saucepans have a squared cross section and are used for basic heating and boiling. **Sauciers** have a tapered cross section and rounded bottom. They are best for preparation of sauces, custards, risotto, and creamy foods, as there are no corners in which food can hide and burn. Their wider mouth is accommodating to whisking.

Skillets have low, flared sides that help with evaporation and steam dissipation. They are useful for browning and/or caramelizing, and for reducing sauces. The sloped sides make it easy to flip food and slide it out when done. **Sauté pans** have straight sides and are lidded. They are used in braising and panfrying, as the high sides reduce splatters and keep in moist heat.

Kitchen lingo

All day: total number of an item on one order, e.g., 2 burgers medium rare + 1 burger medium = 3 burgers all day.

Check the score: tell me the number of tickets that need to be prepared.

Dragging: not ready with the rest of the order, e.g., "the fries are dragging."

Down the Hudson: into the garbage disposal.

Drop: start cooking, e.g., "drop the fries."

Fire: start cooking, but with more urgency, e.g., "fire the burgers."

Get me a runner: get me someone to take this food to a table now.

In the weeds: running behind.

Make it cry: add onions.

The Man: the health inspector (whether male or female).

On a rail or on the fly: with extreme urgency, e.g., "get me two soups on the fly."

Mise en place

Everything needed to prepare a recipe or to be used during a cook's shift—recipes, ingredients, utensils, pots and pans, stocks, sauces, serviceware, and so on—must be planned for, gathered, and pre-prepped before direct preparation begins. *Mise en place* (MEEZ en plahs)—French for "everything in its place"—allows a cook to work in a state of constant readiness without having to stop to find or assemble basic items.

"The universe is in order when your station is set up the way you like it."

—ANTHONY BOURDAIN,
Kitchen Confidential (2000)

We eat with our eyes, nose, ears, and sense of touch.

Before a fork travels to a customer's mouth, he or she has begun to judge it with the eyes (color, variety, arrangement), nose (smell), ears (the sizzle of a hot dish or crunch of a fresh vegetable), and touch (crispness, texture). Studies have indicated that "pre-eating" is nutritious: If a dish looks appealing, the body absorbs more nutrients from it. [Source: *American Journal of Clinical Nutrition*, April 1977]

Yes

No

Shake hands with a knife.

To hold a chef's knife properly, rest your thumb on one side at the juncture of the blade and handle and let your middle, index, and pinky fingers grip the handle naturally on the other side. The forefinger rests on the side of the blade, near the handle. "Choking up" in this way will give you maximum control and minimize strain on the wrist—a critical consideration when working all day in the kitchen.

Never rest your index finger atop the blade, pointing down its length. Although this might seem to lend stability, it actually increases wobbling and robs your strokes of power and accuracy.

Rectangular

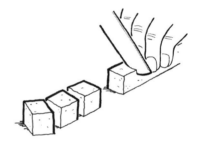

Dice

Basic knife cuts

Rectangular cuts: thin, matchstick-like strips roughly square in cross section, often used for vegetables, meats, or fish in sautéing and stir-frying. Cuts longer than 2-1/2" are usually avoided because they are difficult to fit into the mouth.

Fine Julienne (joo-lee-ENN): 1/16" × 1/16" × 2-1/2" long.

Julienne: 1/8" × 1/8" × 2-1/2" long.

Batonnet (bah-toh-NAY): 1/4" × 1/4" × 2-1/2" long.

Dice cuts: suitable for vegetables such as carrots, celery, onions, root vegetables, and potatoes for use in soups, stews, stocks, and side components.

Brunoise (broo-NWAZ) / small dice: 1/8" × 1/8" × 1/8".

Macédoine (mah-se-DWAN) / medium dice: 1/4" × 1/4" × 1/4".

Parmentier (par-men-ti-AY) / large dice: 1/2" × 1/2" × 1/2".

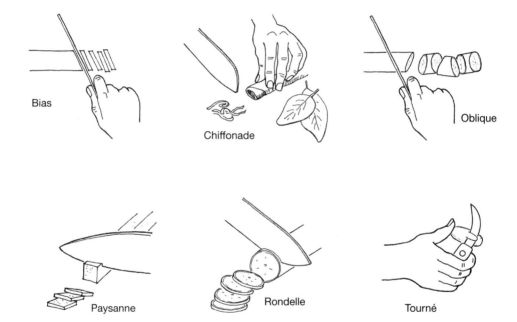

Bias

Chiffonade

Oblique

Paysanne

Rondelle

Tourné

Specialty knife cuts

Bias (BI-as) **or Asian**: a diagonal cut, often used for elongating slices of slender vegetables; greater surface area enables faster cooking.

Chiffonade (chif-oh-NOD): a thin, shred-like cut used for leafy herbs and greens. The leaves are stacked, rolled into a cylinder, and thinly sliced.

Oblique (oh-BLEEK) **or Roll**: made in the manner of a bias cut, but the food is rolled a partial turn between each cut, producing an irregular "V" shape. Used for vegetables in stocks and roasting, as it maximizes surface area.

Paysanne (pie-ZAHN): a flat, square cut, about 1/2" × 1/2" × 1/8" thick. Used most often as a garnish.

Rondelle (ron-DELL): flat, round slices cut from vegetables or fruits, primarily used in soups, salads, and side components.

Tourné (tor-NAY): an aesthetic football- or barrel-shaped cut used for potatoes, carrots, and other root vegetables. 1-1/2" long × 1/2" wide, with six or seven evenly spaced sections around and blunt ends. Tourné means *to turn* in French.

What does a forkful look like?

When creating a dish, don't just think about how the plate will look when delivered to the table; consider how it will appear on the diner's fork or spoon. Do you want the foods served in large pieces to encourage cutting, or should they be small enough for each mouthful to have a blend of flavors? Do you want your soup to have four colorful vegetables in every spoonful? Do you want your salad prepared in a way that encourages three items on every forkful?

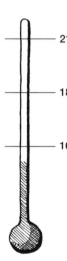

212°F / 100°C: **Boiling.** Recognized by large, highly agitated bubbles.

185°F to 205°F: **Simmering.** Water is slightly agitated, not rolling.

160°F to 180°F: **Poaching.** Water is very hot but has no movement.

How to boil water

1   Fill a comfortably sized pot with a generous amount of water; too much is bet-
    ter than too little. Use cold water, as warm water can contain impurities from
    the water heater. Also, many foods, such as rice, eggs, and root vegetables,
    will cook more evenly from a cold start.
2   Add salt to the water. Adding salt early will help it penetrate the food.
3   Place the pot on the stove and cover with a lid. Don't use a burner or flame
    larger than the pot, as this will waste energy.
4   Water boils at 212°F/100°C at sea level. The boiling point drops 1.8°F/1°C for
    every 1,000-foot increase in altitude.

"Cooking is the oldest, most basic, and most universal human application of physical and chemical changes to natural materials."

—ARTHUR E. GROSSER, *The Cookbook Decoder, or Culinary Alchemy Explained*

Know why customers walk through the door.

Customers seek more from a restaurant than the satisfaction of their appetites: value, comfort, serenity, prestige, companionship, relaxation, humor, artistry, to be anonymous, to impress a companion, to watch the big game, to see and be seen.

A good chef understands and helps staff understand the many reasons customers choose a restaurant, and makes clear what should be done to meet their needs. If the clientele is inclined to visit for value, create an impression of abundance on the plate and keep water glasses and bread baskets full. If guests arrive in search of artistry, go the extra step in plating techniques. If they seek a family atmosphere, keep the lights up, have at least three kid-sized choices on the menu, and prepare staff to take spills and tantrums in stride.

Keep guests informed.

Communication between the front of the house (the dining room) and the back (the kitchen) is key to satisfying customers. Be honest with customers about errors and oversights. If a dish is running late, inform the guest immediately, before he or she inquires about the status of the order. Customers will usually accept mistakes—and might even consider them part of the fun of the dining experience—if they feel their needs have otherwise been anticipated. Sweat the details, but most of all make sure the overall experience is enjoyable.

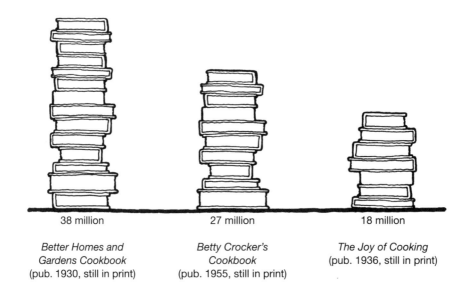

38 million

27 million

18 million

*Better Homes and
Gardens Cookbook*
(pub. 1930, still in print)

*Betty Crocker's
Cookbook*
(pub. 1955, still in print)

The Joy of Cooking
(pub. 1936, still in print)

Estimated sales, all-time bestselling cookbooks

The oldest cookbook

The world's oldest surviving cookbook is *De Re Coquinaria* ("On Cookery"). Most of the recipes are attributed to Marcus Gavius Apicius, a first century Roman. The book was compiled a hundred or more years after his death.

"No one who cooks, cooks alone. Even at her most solitary, a cook in the kitchen is surrounded by generations of cooks past, the advice and menus of cooks present, the wisdom of cookbook writers."

—LAURIE COLWIN, writer (1944–1992)

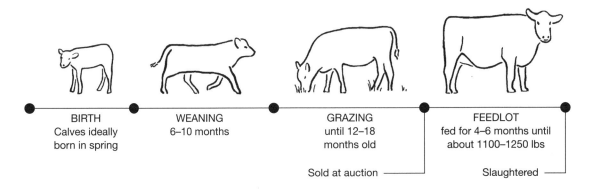

BIRTH
Calves ideally
born in spring

WEANING
6–10 months

GRAZING
until 12–18
months old

Sold at auction ———

FEEDLOT
fed for 4–6 months until
about 1100–1250 lbs

Slaughtered ———

Common timeline for commercial beef

19

Good beef is 30 days old.

Beef is aged to allow an animal's natural enzymes to break down tough connective tissues, resulting in deeper flavor and improved texture. **Dry aging** needs at least 11 days and may take more than 30 days. The meat is hung and exposed to climate controlled air, where it loses 15 to 30% of its weight, mostly due to water evaporation, becomes meatier and more buttery, and develops a more concentrated flavor. Dry aged beef is rarely found in supermarkets.

Wet aging takes 5 to 7 days and is less expensive. The beef is sealed in plastic in its own juices (e.g., Cryovaced), making it convenient for shipping. Flavor is milder than dry-aged beef.

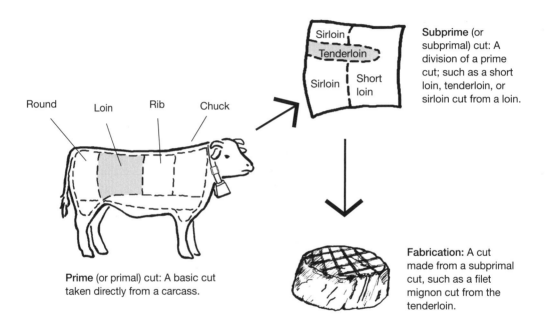

Round   Loin   Rib   Chuck

Sirloin

Tenderloin

Sirloin   Short loin

Subprime (or subprimal) cut: A division of a prime cut; such as a short loin, tenderloin, or sirloin cut from a loin.

Prime (or primal) cut: A basic cut taken directly from a carcass.

Fabrication: A cut made from a subprimal cut, such as a filet mignon cut from the tenderloin.

The primal (or prime) cuts of meat

A carcass is processed by quartering. It is split in half down the backbone, and then into forequarters and hindquarters. The quarters are then carved into the primal cuts sold to butchers, retailers, and restaurants, who create the smaller cuts found on shelves, menus, and plates. The primal cuts most used in restaurant service are:

20

Chuck: about 28% of carcass weight. A flavorful cut, but with many connective tissues, calling for moist or combination cooking. Not used as much as other prime cuts in food service. In veal and lamb, it is called shoulder; in pork, shoulder butt.

Rib: about 10% of carcass weight. Heavily marbled and very tender. Suited to dry or combination cooking. In veal, lamb, and pork, it is called rack.

Loin: short loin and sirloin together make up 15% of the carcass. Very tender; most of the popular and expensive cuts come from the loin. Excellent for roasting.

Round: 24% of carcass weight. Very flavorful, moderate connective tissues, best roasted/braised. Called leg in veal, lamb, and pork.

USDA prime and the "other" prime

USDA inspection is financed by the beef industry and is performed upon request of cattle producers and meat packers. Grading is based on marbling (distributed flecks and streaks of fat; more marbling means more tender, juicy, and flavorful) and age (flavor and texture are best in cattle between 18 and 24 months).

USDA Prime: The top grade, awarded to only 2% of all graded beef. Rare in supermarkets, sold mostly to restaurants. Fine grained with high (8 to 11%) marbling. It is important to note that meats not graded by the USDA as Prime are sometimes called "prime" by providers and restaurants, but only a full label of "USDA Prime" indicates the highest quality.

USDA Choice: 4 to 7% marbling. More than half of all graded beef is labeled Choice.

USDA Select: 3 to 4% marbling, about a third of all graded meat. Popular at retail for its leanness, but generally the lowest grade of steak in restaurants.

Standard, Commercial, Utility, Cutter, and Canner grades: the lowest grades, used in meat pies, meat sticks, and potted meats.

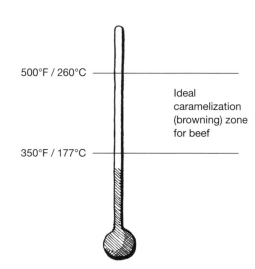

500°F / 260°C —

350°F / 177°C —

Ideal
caramelization
(browning) zone
for beef

Searing meat doesn't "seal in the juices."

Contrary to popular belief, searing meat at a high temperature does not create a barrier that locks in its natural juices. Searing *can* produce a very juicy product, but this comes from cooking quickly at a high temperature, as opposed to grilling or sautéing for a longer time at a lower temperature. Some studies even suggest that a seared piece of meat may have less moisture than one cooked at a lower temperature. Further, the tasty crust produced by searing may make the mouth water more, producing the impression of a juicier result.

The purpose of searing is to promote a *Maillard Reaction*, which browns the outside surface of a steak by caramelizing its natural sugars and amino acids, producing a crisp and flavorful crust. The ideal temperature zone for caramelizing is 350°F to 500°F. At temperatures over 500°F, the surface may char, producing a burned taste as well as cancer causing agents.

Use one spoon for cooking and a
second spoon for tasting.

23

Look, smell, poke, cut, taste.

A novice chef can be overreliant on recipes, and might even serve a dish he or she has not tasted. But don't cook a dish for the 20 minutes called for in a recipe and assume it is done; the oven might not have been calibrated correctly, the food might be of a different density than assumed by the recipe, and innumerable other unforeseen factors might affect cooking times. Instead, make regular visual checks to verify brownness. Put a fork in it. Check internal temperatures with a meat thermometer. Use your sense of smell. And don't forget to taste it!

1. Meet the tip of varying numbers of fingers to the thumb on the same hand.

Rare: Use a relaxed hand (don't touch fingers to thumb).

Medium rare: Touch index finger to thumb.

Medium: Touch first 2 fingers to thumb.

Medium well: Touch 3 fingers to thumb.

Well done: Touch all 4 fingers to thumb.

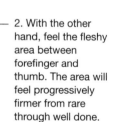

2. With the other hand, feel the fleshy area between forefinger and thumb. The area will feel progressively firmer from rare through well done.

The hand test for recognizing doneness in beef

Recognizing doneness in meat

24

A good cook can visually and intuitively recognize done-ness levels in meat—an important skill when test-tasting or cutting into a food is prohibited. Developing this skill takes much trial and error. In beef steaks:

Rare: interior of steak is very red and slightly warm.

Medium rare: interior of steak is red and fully warm.

Medium: interior of steak is red with some pink surround, and hot.

Medium well: interior of steak is pink and hot.

Well done: interior of steak is grayish brown and fully hot.

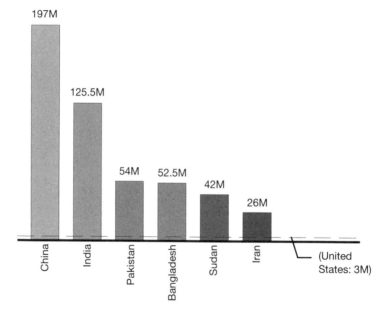

World leaders in goat population

Source: foodreference.com

25

Goat is the most popular meat in the world.

The transition from nomadic hunter-gatherer to agricultural societies began around 10,000 BCE. Early farmers discovered that goats provided many resources—fur, milk, and meat—in a small package that was easy to transport and feed. Goats also reproduce quickly, making it easy to grow a herd. They thus became the first animal to be domesticated for food.

Round fish

Body is oval or round in cross section, and the eyes are on opposite sides of the head. Includes bass, catfish, cod, pike, salmon, snapper, tuna, and trout. Provides multiple steaks or two fillets.

Flatfish

Flat body allows it to swim near the ocean floor. Born with eyes laterally located, one migrates to the top of the body. Includes Dover sole, flounder, monkfish, and halibut. Provides four fillets.

Two categories of fish

Fresh fish smells like the water it came from. Old fish smells like fish.

26

- Fresh fish looks and smells clean and has a sweet, water-like scent, with no slime, cuts, or bruises. The fins should be pliable.
- Fish scales should not be loose. Run your fingers across the scales; if they separate easily, it is not fresh.
- There should be some tightness and resistance when you press gently on the meat of the fish.
- The eyes should be clear and clean, and not sunken below the head.
- The gills should be bright pink or maroon, not deep red.
- Check for "belly burn," a dark reddish, bloodlike stain on the skin, which indicates that the viscera were left in the fish too long, resulting in bacteria growth.

27

The freshest shrimp might be frozen shrimp.

Nearly all shrimp are flash frozen at sea because of their short shelf-life. When non-frozen shrimp are offered for sale, they probably aren't fresh but were frozen at one time and later thawed. Buying frozen is safer, cheaper, and more convenient.

If a lobster dies shortly before cooking, cook it anyway.
If the tail and claw meat remain firm and smell sweet
and fresh, use it to make lobster bisque or soufflé. If
the meat is mushy or cottage cheese-like, discard it.

28

Don't drown a lobster.

Don't keep lobsters in a cooler full of ice; when the ice melts, the lobster will drown in the fresh water. Instead, place cold, wet newspapers or towels over them until they are ready to be cooked. They can stay alive this way in a refrigerator for several days to a week. Alternately, you can place the lobsters in a perforated pan with ice, and place another pan under it to catch the water.

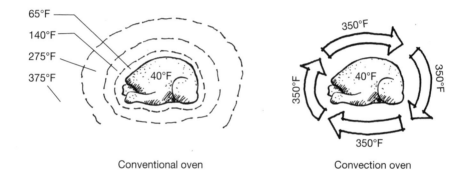

65°F

140°F

275°F

375°F

40°F

Conventional oven

350°F

350°F

350°F

350°F

40°F

Convection oven

Why convection ovens are faster

29

In conventional ovens, the air immediately adjacent to the food is cooler than the rest of the oven because the food is cooler. A convection oven rapidly circulates air, continually disrupting the cooler air, and keeping the food in contact with the ideal cooking temperature. Additionally, convection helps guard against a lower temperature near the door, a common characteristic of conventional ovens. The result is faster, more even cooking at 25 to 50 degrees below the temperature required by a conventional oven.

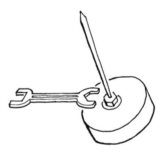

1

2

How to calibrate a thermometer

30

Kitchen thermometers should be calibrated at least once a week or whenever dropped. To calibrate:

1   Fill a glass with crushed ice. Add cold water and stir thoroughly. Insert the thermometer without touching the side or bottom of the glass.
2   When the mercury has stopped moving (usually about 30 seconds) and without removing the stem from the ice, turn the calibration nut under the head so the pointer points to 32°F/0°C.

A thermometer also can be calibrated using boiling water and adjusting the thermometer to the boiling point at your altitude.

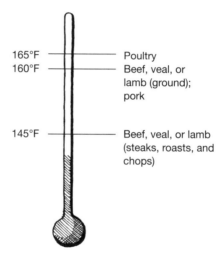

165°F — Poultry
160°F — Beef, veal, or lamb (ground); pork
145°F — Beef, veal, or lamb (steaks, roasts, and chops)

USDA recommended temperatures

31

Internal temperatures for meat

Cooking meats to the recommended minimum temperatures will help ensure proper done-ness and guard against harmful bacteria. Remove the meat from the heat source when the internal temperature is slightly lower than that shown, to allow for carryover cooking.

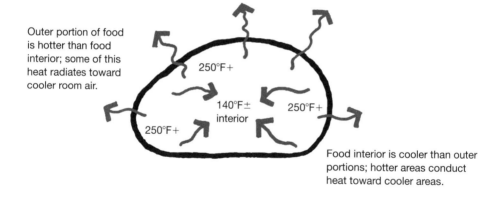

70°F room air

Outer portion of food is hotter than food interior; some of this heat radiates toward cooler room air.

250°F+

140°F± interior

250°F+

250°F+

Food interior is cooler than outer portions; hotter areas conduct heat toward cooler areas.

Food can get hotter *after* cooking.

Overcooking is a common error of the inexperienced cook. This is partly due to a fear of serving undercooked food, and also because food continues to cook after being removed from the heat source. During carryover cooking, the internal temperature of a food continues rising for several minutes after being removed from the heat source, as heat from the food's warmer outside (which was closest to the heat source) continues moving toward the cooler inside.

For meats, cooking should be halted when the internal temperature is lower than the target temperature. Monitor the internal temperature during carryover cooking, allowing about 5 to10 additional minutes for small and medium cuts, and more for very large cuts. (Whole poultry and fish behave slightly differently due to the internal cavity.) This additional time also allows the proteins to relax, so that juices expelled during cooking can be reabsorbed.

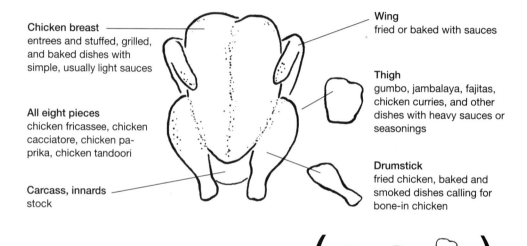

32

Chicken breast
entrees and stuffed, grilled, and baked dishes with simple, usually light sauces

All eight pieces
chicken fricassee, chicken cacciatore, chicken paprika, chicken tandoori

Carcass, innards
stock

Wing
fried or baked with sauces

Thigh
gumbo, jambalaya, fajitas, chicken curries, and other dishes with heavy sauces or seasonings

Drumstick
fried chicken, baked and smoked dishes calling for bone-in chicken

(drumstick + thigh = whole leg)

Buy it whole and cut it up.

Fabricating a chicken into eight pieces is as simple as following the structure of the bird and finding the bones.

33

Wings: face the rear of the bird toward you. Remove the wings at the joint closest to the body. When serving French, Supreme, or Airline style breasts, leave the first wing bone attached to the breast, and sever the wing at the middle joint. The wing meat can be left as is, or pushed toward the breast.

Legs: pull a leg and thigh away from the breast and cut through toward the thigh joint. Bend the leg toward you and twist until the thighbone pops out of joint. Cut below and around, following the carcass, and remove. Repeat other side.

Drums and thighs: separate the drum from the thigh by feeling where the joints meet on the inside. Place the whole leg skin-side down. Cut straight through between the joints.

Breast: following the line of the breastbone, carve out the breast meat on each side, cutting close to the carcass.

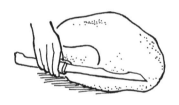

1

2

Undercut a poultry breast before slicing it.

34

To slice a poultry breast into even, controlled pieces, allow the bird to cool for five to ten minutes after cooking. This will make the meat firmer and more receptive to thin slicing.

To cut, first make a deep horizontal cut at the base of the breast, just above the wing, all the way to the carcass. Then slice the breast thinly and evenly in a downward direction. The pieces will fall off cleanly without tearing away from the bird.

The kitchen brigade

The *brigade de cuisine* system of kitchen operations common today was created by French chef Auguste Escoffier (1846–1935). A brigade typically includes:

Executive chef: responsible for all kitchen operations, supplies, equipment, dealing with vendors, training and coordinating staff, designing the menu and recipes, and creating the atmosphere of the restaurant. Also the chief expeditor.

Sous-chef: second in charge in the kitchen, reports to the executive chef. Typically hires and schedules personnel, may act as expeditor during food service.

35

Expeditor: performs the final check on all prepared dishes, wipes smudges, and coordinates with servers.

Line cooks: have the ability to work at every cooking station.

Station chefs: in charge of specialized stations such as sauté, grill, fish, fry, roast, and vegetables.

Garde manger (gard mon-ZHAY): a station chef specializing in cold foods, including salads, cold entrees, charcuterie, and raw bar.

Prep cook: measures ingredients, prepares vegetables, fruits, and salads, cuts meat and seafood for cooks, monitors soups and sauces.

Pastry chef: responsible for breads, pastries, and desserts.

In large recipes, measure salt by weight, as volume measurements will vary widely depending on type and manufacturer. A cup of table salt weighs about 10 ounces, while a cup of kosher salt weighs 5 to 8 ounces.

The four salts in a kitchen

Salt contains sodium and chloride, minerals craved by our bodies. Food that doesn't contain some salt rarely tastes right. Salts commonly used in kitchens include:

Table salt: a highly refined salt from which undesired minerals have been removed. It may be fortified with iodine to compensate for its loss during processing. Some brands contain calcium silicate, an anti-caking ingredient that can impart a metallic taste. It is preferred in baking, as its fine granules promote consistent measurement.

36

Kosher salt: a coarse salt evaporated from brine, in a manner approved by the Orthodox Jewish faith. It contains no additives. Its coarse texture makes it easy to pinch with the fingers and sprinkle onto foods.

Sea salt: evaporated from sea water, it has the strongest flavor. Costlier than table or kosher salt, and available in coarse or fine grains. Most types are gray; pink, brown, and black varieties are also available.

Rock salt: large unrefined crystals with a grayish hue. Not for eating, but often used as a presentation bed for oysters and clams.

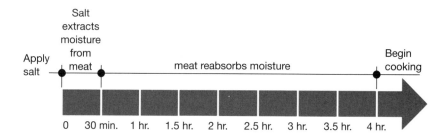

Salt
extracts
moisture
from
meat

Apply
salt

meat reabsorbs moisture

Begin
cooking

0   30 min.   1 hr.   1.5 hr.   2 hr.   2.5 hr.   3 hr.   3.5 hr.   4 hr.

Salting of meats

When and when not to add salt

Salt meats 1 to 4 hours before cooking. For the first half hour or so after salting, salt extracts moisture from meat. After that, the protein fibers loosen up and take back the salty juices. The cooked product ends up more tender, flavorful, and juicy, with a crisp tasty crust. **Brining** (1/2 cup salt per gallon of water) works similarly. Through osmosis, the salt alters the meat cells structurally, allowing more water to be absorbed.

37

Don't salt immediately before deep-frying. The salt will alter the surface of the food, and it won't fry as crisply as it should.

Don't salt stocks while preparing them, as subsequent reduction can make them too salty. Also be careful with sauces that may be reduced later.

Salt the liquid when blanching. Don't wait until flash reheating to add salt; salt the liquid before boiling the food to enhance color, flavor, and crispness.

Salt during cooking, not just at the end. Salt helps heighten and blend other flavors. Adding salt early in the cooking process gives you a better opportunity to evaluate and adjust the dish.

Salt after boiling begins but before adding food when boiling in an aluminum or cast iron pot to prevent pitting of the pot material.

Ten mistakes of the inexperienced cook

- Improper or inadequate *mise en place.*
- Poor timing, resulting in foods not being completed in the proper sequence.
- Not reading or knowing the recipe before starting.
- Inadequate or too much heat, particularly in preparing proteins.
- Using the wrong cut of meat for the dish or method of cooking.
- Overcrowding the pan when sautéing or baking.
- Cooking starches in a too-small pot, resulting in clumping.
- Overcooking due to not allowing for carryover cooking or because of a fear of serving undercooked food.
- Not using enough salt or not salting at the proper time in the cooking process.
- Not tasting a dish before serving it.

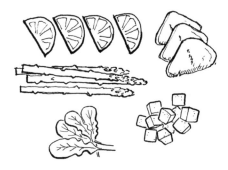

Shape counterpoints

Eight ways to make a plate look better

1 **Use negative space.** Group food to create an illusion of abundance, but don't crowd the plate. Create a wide border by centering or offsetting the food.
2 **Avoid flatness.** Arrange or shingle food at different heights. But be careful with stacking, as food needs to stay stacked. Use food molds to bind rice and grains.
3 **Use white plates for simplicity.** Colored plates can be effective attention-getters as long as they don't overwhelm the food. Likewise, coordinate the type of food with plate textures and colors, such as country cuisine with rustic plates.
4 **Use different plate shapes.** If round plates seem too predictable, try square, triangular, or oblong, keeping an eye on the creation of negative space.
5 **Use strong geometries.** Play clear geometries off random arrangements.
6 **Use counterpoints.** Vary shapes, colors, textures, and arrangements so that each food makes the others more appealing. A long green vegetable, such as green beans or asparagus, is a dependable counterpoint to many foods.
7 **Add a garnish.** Use a contrasting color and texture, and try not to make it superfluous—a garnish should be intended to be eaten.
8 **Paint the sauce.** Use a pastry brush to paint an elegant, dramatic stroke of sauce or a ladle to create a ring of color in the negative space of the plate.

39

1. Add a small amount of stock, water, or wine to a pan containing bits of "fond" after cooking.

2. Gently dislodge the fond with a wooden spoon.

3. Heat until the liquid is reduced to the desired consistency.

Deglazing

Focus the flavor.

Flavor is the culmination of everything experienced in a dish—color, texture, aroma, even sound. To enhance flavor experience, try:

Counterpointing: use salt to subdue bitter and sour tones and bring out sweetness. Use sweet, cool, or creamy foods to counterpoint spicy foods, such as mango salsa with spicy jerk chicken, or cool sour cream with five-alarm chili. Add crunchy foods to counterpoint creamy, tart foods to counterpoint smoky flavors, and acidic foods to counterpoint fatty dishes.

40

Intensifying: reduce (evaporate) liquid from a stock or sauce to deepen its flavor. Or deglaze the pan after cooking, by using *fond (*caramelized bits of food left in the pan) to make a flavorful sauce.

Salting: adding salt early in cooking allows deeper infusion of flavor compared to salting after cooking.

Moderating: to keep strong-flavored foods from dominating other flavors in the same dish, blanch or partially cook them separately and add them to the main dish at the last minute.

A sauce is only as good as its stock.

Stocks are the basis for many sauces, soups, stews, gravies, and glacés. **White stock** is made from the bones of fish, chicken, or veal, or from vegetables only. **Brown stocks** are derived from veal, duck, turkey, poultry, rabbit, or other bones that have been previously browned in the oven. Browned bones produce the most flavorful stock.

41

To make stock, use 5 quarts of cold water and 1 pound of vegetables (called *mirepoix* in French, and *sofrito* in Spanish and Italian; typically 50% onions, 25% celery and 25% carrots) for every 5 pounds of bones. Substitute leeks or parsnips for carrots in white stocks so the stock doesn't get too orange.

Seasonings typically consist of bay leaf, peppercorns, garlic, and parsley. They may be wrapped in a sachet (a small bag made of cheesecloth) before being placed in the stock pot.

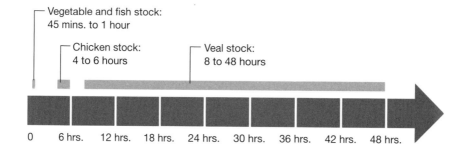

Simmering times for stock

Don't boil stock.

42

Boiling recirculates impurities and makes stock cloudy. Maintain a gentle simmer throughout, and regularly skim impurities as they rise to the top.

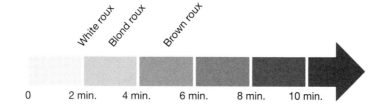

White roux Blond roux Brown roux

0   2 min.   4 min.   6 min.   8 min.   10 min.

Heating times

Roux: the longer, the darker

Roux is a thickener used in soups and sauces. To make roux, heat butter, lard, or other fat in a saucepan and slowly add an equal weight of flour. Stir gently and continuously until the flour granules evenly absorb the fat and produce an evenly textured paste. The longer a roux is heated, the more the flour taste will be reduced and the darker it will be. For a few tablespoons of roux:

White roux: heat briefly, about 1 to 2 minutes, only until bubbles develop on the surface. Use for thickening white sauces.

Blond or pale roux: heat 3 to 4 minutes to a blond or pale color. Suitable for lighter sauces used with chicken and fish entrees.

Brown roux: heat for 5 to 8 minutes or longer, until dark brown. Use for thickening brown sauces such as Espagnole. In southern cooking, pan drippings are often used.

When blending roux with stock to create a sauce or soup, gradually add hot stock to the roux (not the other way around), and whisk continually.

43

Marie-Antoine Carême (1784–1833)

Five mother sauces

Marie-Antoine Carême, considered the founder of classical French cuisine, streamlined many cooking techniques. He made mother sauces in large quantities, then created daughter sauces by adding spices, herbs, and/or wine. Auguste Escoffier later added tomato, vinaigrette, and other sauces to Carême's initial four mother sauces.

Béchamel (cream) sauce: base of milk and white roux. Suited to pasta, fish, and chicken. Daughter sauces include Mornay, Nantua, Soubise, and Mustard.

Veloute (white) sauce: base of white stock and blond roux. Good for fish and chicken entrees. Daughter sauces include Poulette, Aurora, Curry, Mushroom, and Albufera.

44

Espagnole (brown) sauce: base of brown stock and brown roux, suitable for poultry and meat. Daughter sauces include Bordelaise, Robert, Chasseur, and Madeira.

Tomato sauce: tomato base, used for pasta, poultry, and meat entrees. Can be flavored by rib bones, sausage, and other meats. Daughter sauces include Bolognese, Creole, and Portuguese.

Hollandaise (butter) sauce: base of clarified butter, egg yolk, and lemon juice. Suited to Eggs Benedict and vegetables. Daughter sauces include Maltaise, Mousseline, Noisette, and Girondine.

Auguste Escoffier (1846–1935)

"Among the faithful, in the great kitchens of the world, Escoffier is to Carême what the New Testament is to the Old."

—ANDRÉ SIMON (1877–1970),
A Concise Encyclopedia of Gastronomy (1952)

45

1. Cut cold butter into small cubes.

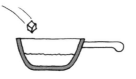

2. Add one cube at a time to a sauce once it's stopped cooking.

3. Whisk steadily, adding butter until the desired consistency is achieved.

Mount with butter to perfect the sauce.

Monter au beurre (mon-tay o BURR, French for "to mount with butter") is the addition of a few ounces of cold, unsalted butter at the end of cooking a sauce to give it a velvety texture and rich sheen. The proteins in the butter act as an emulsifier, giving the whole flavor a greater sum than the parts. In larger quantities, the butter acts as a thickener.

46

1. Melt butter in a heavy saucepan over medium heat. Water in the butter will evaporate and milk solids will settle at the bottom.

2. Pour or ladle the clarified portion of the butter into another container and discard the milk solids.

Clarified butter

Clarified butter is butter that has had the milk solids removed from it. It can be stored longer and heated to a higher temperature without burning than regular butter. One pound of regular butter produces 12 liquid ounces of clarified butter. Clarified butter is rarely or never used in baking, as the milk solids in regular butter help baked goods cohere.

Clarified butter is called *sman* in Middle Eastern cooking and *ghee* in Indian cooking. In both, the butter is heated until the solids brown, and then strained, yielding a dark, nutty taste.

47

Menu types

Static menu: offers the same dishes daily to guests for an extended period of time. Common at fast food establishments and chain restaurants. A static menu may be combined with daily specials, and may change seasonally.

Cycle menu: changes daily (a Monday menu, a Tuesday menu, etc.) and repeats every week. Common in schools, hospitals, penitentiaries, etc.

Market menu: based on what is currently available for purchase by the restaurant, suggesting extensive use of fresh products and seasonal variation.

Farm-to-table menu: focuses solely on fresh, local/regional (usually 100 miles or less), sustainable, and often organic ingredients. May change daily according to types and quantities of available foods.

A hybrid menu combines some or all of the preceding.

Checklist for writing a recipe

- ☐ Name of dish
- ☐ Total yield, individual portion size, and total portions
- ☐ List of ingredients, with exact amount of each
- ☐ Special equipment, if any
- ☐ Special *mise en place* procedures
- ☐ Step by step directions, including preparation time, cooking time, and temperatures
- ☐ Plating: type of plate, amount per serving, side components, how arranged, garnish, etc.
- ☐ Recommended wine pairing
- ☐ Storage and reuse of leftover components

A menu is only as good as a chef's ability to write a recipe.

A team prepares the many dishes offered on a menu; a successful team effort begins with clear recipes. When writing recipes, don't include only ingredients, but equipment, method, temperature, time, yield, garnish, dishes, presentation, wine recommendation, and storage and reuse of leftovers. If a chef has difficulty translating a dish into a recipe that cooks can follow, it shouldn't be on the menu.

Make sure the ingredients in every dish will be available for the duration of the menu. Contact suppliers to verify prices, availability, and quality. The most reliable source may be a compromise of these three factors.

Finally, share the new dish with everyone involved in food service at the restaurant. Give all an opportunity to taste, question, and evaluate.

49

Menu-plan for leftovers.

Efficient ordering and use of food ties directly to a restaurant's bottom line. Make sure every perishable food item has more than one place on your menu, so that if one dish goes unordered it will be consumed in another. Have a planned leftover use for every dish, for example as a lunch or specials item. Additionally:

- Save carcasses and bones for making stocks.
- Save meat and fish scraps for soups, stews, chowders, meat loafs, meatballs, *amuse-bouche*, and charcuterie.
- Save vegetable scraps and stems from chopped herbs to flavor stocks or for use in purees.
- Use stale bread for breading, stuffing, and croutons.

Mignardise (mee-nyar-deez) are small sweets
presented after a meal, also as a gift.

Amuse-bouche is a gift from the chef.

Amuse-bouche literally means mouth amuser. Presenting this bite-sized appetizer to customers awakens the taste buds prior to the dining experience, and is a way for a chef to express his aesthetic ambitions without overwhelming the diner or dining experience. It is often served on a spoon.

51

Stir-fry is a form of sautéing that uses a wok.

When sautéing, make it *jump*.

Sautéing is a simple, elegant cooking art using a very hot pan. In French, sauté means *jump*; the pan should be hot enough to cause food placed in it to jump or pop.

- Good *mise en place* is essential; have all food products fully prepared and chopped before beginning to cook. Make sure the food is dry.
- Don't use a non-stick pan. The pan should be large, as crowding will minimize contact of food with the heat source and cause moisture to build up, preventing caramelization.
- Heat the pan without oil, until a few drops of water tossed on it sizzle.
- Place a small amount of fat (oil or butter) in the pan and continue heating. You can tell the pan is hot enough by tossing a small piece of onion into it. If it jumps, it's ready.
- Add dry food to the pan and keep it moving fast. Root vegetables such as carrots take the longest to cook. Put mushrooms, shrimp, scallops, and mussels in later so they don't get rubbery.
- It's better to do a pan flip than to use a spatula. Flipping turns more food at the same time, promoting more even cooking.

52

1. Boil the vegetable in water or stock, or steam it. Stop cooking a few minutes before fully done, when the color turns vivid.

2. Shock with an ice water bath or cold running water. (Use tongs to remove the food if you want to reuse the hot water.)

3. Drain and store until needed. Before serving, perform a "flash" boil or sauté.

Blanching

Boil, shock, drain!

Blanching is a simple process that quickly arrests cooking, enhances the flavor and color of many vegetables, including asparagus, broccoli, cauliflower, and green beans, and improves timeliness.

53

Crisphead   Romaine   Butterhead   Leaf

Rip, don't cut salad greens.

Except for Romaine, lettuce fares better when ripped than when cut. Tearing encourages breakage along naturally occurring cellular fault lines, while cutting damages cells, producing bruising and browning.

54

Failproof balsamic vinaigrette
1 part vinegar
3 to 4 parts oil
1/4 part emulsifier

How to keep salad dressing from separating

Emulsification is the combining, through rapid agitation, of two immiscible (unmixable) liquids to create a new liquid. Emulsified liquids tend to separate over time, as one experiences with vinaigrette and other salad dressings. This problem can be solved by adding an emulsifier, such as egg yolk, mayonnaise, yogurt, ground nuts, mustard, or fruit puree, the molecules of which are friendly to both water and fats.

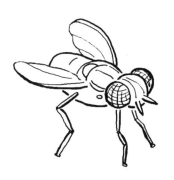

55

Pesticides

The fruits and vegetables most likely to have pesticide residue are peaches, apples, nectarines, strawberries, cherries, imported grapes, pears, raspberries, sweet bell peppers, celery, kale, spinach, lettuce, and carrots. The least likely to have residue are onions, sweet corn, asparagus, sweet peas, cabbage, eggplant, broccoli, tomatoes, and sweet potatoes. [Source: Consumers Union]

To remove pesticides, bacteria, and dirt from the surface of smooth skinned vegetables and fruits, mix one part lemon juice or white or distilled vinegar to three parts tap water. Apply with a spray bottle and let sit for one minute. Rinse with cool water and dry completely before storing.

56

Small local farms can produce more food per acre than large corporate farms.

A typical restaurant dinner travels hundreds or even thousands of miles by the time it reaches the table. It may have been genetically modified for firmness and color (often at the expense of flavor), or treated with steroids, pesticides, or radiation.

The sustainable agriculture movement promotes simpler, more organic, more localized methods of food production. Studies suggest that small local farms actually produce more food per acre than large corporate farms, because small farmers know their land so well they can maximize every odd corner of it and work it by hand if needed. [Source: Centre for the Environment and Society, University of Essex]

57

Don't buy on the first pass.

Restaurants rely on many suppliers: large corporations for staples, farmers markets for produce, and local independents for mushrooms, seafood, truffles, and other specialties. When shopping at a farmers market:

- **Arrive early** for the best selection; arrive late for the best values.
- **Make two passes** among the vendors before buying. Use your first walkthrough to check quality and taste, ask questions, make notes, and menuplan.
- **Bargain with vendors**. Ask politely, "What are you asking for your [food]?" "What will you take for the remainder of the lug?" or "How much if I take five pounds of each?"
- **Develop a relationship** with trusted vendors and return to them often.

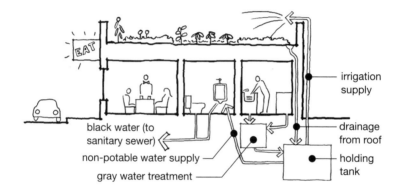

58

EAT

irrigation
supply

black water (to
sanitary sewer)

drainage
from roof

non-potable water supply

holding
tank

gray water treatment

Gray water recycling

Nine ways to make a restaurant more green

- Cultivate relationships with local farmers and suppliers. Minimize the use of foods that are locally out of season.
- Choose certified organic fish, and meats/poultry that do not contain hormones or antibiotics, are free range, and given vegetarian feed.
- Plant an herb or vegetable garden behind the restaurant or on the roof. Teach the neighborhood kids to help maintain it. If permissible, have a small farm and raise your own livestock.
- Maintain a composting pile.
- Install a plumbing system that recycles gray water and runoff from the roof and site. In restrooms, use waterless urinals and touchless sink sensors.
- Purchase furnishings that are used or made from recycled or renewable materials.
- Donate leftovers to food banks and homeless shelters where permitted.
- Recycle old cooking oil for use as biodiesel fuel.
- Create a full recycling program for plastic, glass, paper, metal, and foam products. Make sure take-out containers, plates, and utensils are 100% recyclable. Stock reusable hand towels and napkins when possible.

59

Keeping kosher

Kosher refers to food that meets kashrut, the Jewish dietary law set forth in the Torah. It allows the preparation and consumption of:

- Animals that have split hooves and chew their cud (cattle, goat, sheep, deer, antelope, bison), and any products derived from them, including their milk, organs, and fat, except for fat around vital organs.
- Birds except scavengers and birds of prey. All slaughter of birds or animals must abide by Jewish law, and blood must be drained or broiled out of it entirely.
- Fish that have both scales and fins.
- Fruits and vegetables, if inspected for bugs. Wines and grape products are allowed only if prepared by a Jewish person.

60

The following are not allowed:

- Pigs, rabbits, dogs, or horses, including their flesh, organs, or milk.
- Shellfish, including lobsters, oysters, shrimp, clams, and crabs.
- The blood of any animal.

Meat and dairy cannot be eaten together. Utensils, cookware, and plates used with hot foods that have come into contact with non-kosher food may not be used with kosher food, and vice versa.

Keeping halal

Halal means permissible. The Qur'an allows Muslims to eat what is "pure, clean, nourishing, and pleasing," and prohibits the following:

- an animal that was improperly slaughtered (by strangulation or blunt force) or already dead (i.e., not killed for food)
- an animal not killed in the name of Allah (God)
- carnivorous animals, birds of prey, and land animals without external ears
- blood
- swine (pork)
- intoxicating drinks
- meat from which wild animals have eaten
- meat of an animal that has been sacrificed to idols

61

Hindu food practices

Hindus believe in the interconnection of mind, body, and spirit, and favor food thought not to slow down physical or spiritual growth.

Tamasic foods are considered least desirable. They are deemed to benefit neither mind nor body and to produce anger, greed, and other negative emotions. Example foods include meat, onions, alcohol, and spoiled, fermented, overripe, or otherwise impure foods.

Rajasic foods are believed to benefit the body, but can result in a restlessness or overstimulation of the mind. They include very hot, spicy, salty, bitter, and sour foods, such as chocolate, coffee, tea, eggs, peppers, pickles, and processed foods.

62

Sattvic foods are held to be balancing to the body, purifying to the mind, and calming to the spirit. The most desirable category of food, it includes grains, nuts, fruits, vegetables, milk, clarified butter, and cheese.

Pork is prohibited, as are cows, which are considered sacred. Milk and dairy products are acceptable.

All vegans are vegetarian; not all vegetarians are vegan.

Vegetarians eat no meat, fish, shellfish, or poultry, but will sometimes eat dairy products or eggs (known as lacto-ovo vegetarians).

Semi-vegetarians eat fish and sometimes poultry.

Vegans eat no meat, fish, shellfish, or poultry, or any products from animals, including milk, cheese, and eggs.

All groups typically eat grains, legumes, seeds, nuts, fruits, soy-based products such as soymilk, and limited amounts of concentrated fats, oils, and sugars.

63

To keep a restaurant vegan/vegetarian ready:
- When performing *mise en place*, do not mix meats and vegetables.
- Regardless of what is on the menu, always have a few vegan/vegetarian recipes ready, or know which dishes can be readily and safely altered.
- Get to know your vegan/vegetarian customers and let them know which items on your menu can be made their way.

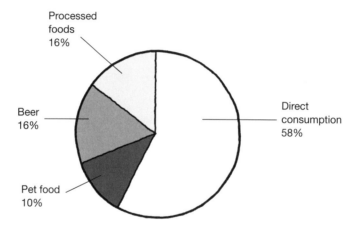

Processed
foods
16%

Beer
16%

Pet food
10%

Direct
consumption
58%

Domestic use of rice grown in the United States
Source: USDA

Rice: the shorter, the stickier.

Long-grain (Indica) is a versatile, popular rice. The grains remain firm and fluffy, after cooking and separate easily. Used in rice pilaf, fried rice, and steamed rice, but not suitable for risotto. Varieties include:

- **Basmati:** extremely aromatic. Grown in the Himalayan foothills, popular in Indian and Middle Eastern cuisines.
- **Carolina or Southern:** the most common rice in the U.S. Not aromatic.
- **Jasmine:** aromatic. Used in pilafs and Asian-style fried rice.

Short- and medium-grain (Japonica) rice is starchy, tender, and sticky, and is good for risotto, sushi, and paella, but isn't recommended for pilaf or fried rice.

- **Arborio:** a round, medium-grain rice with a mild flavor. Used primarily for risotto.
- **Calrose:** a fat, round rice, commonly used in sushi in the United States.

64

Specialty rices include:

- **Brown:** the whole grain of rice from which only the husk has been removed. Has a nutty, hearty taste. Requires more water and twice the cooking time of other rice.
- **Wild:** although, like rice, it is the seed of a type of grass, it is not actually a member of the rice family. Dark brown or black with a nutty aroma and flavor. Takes three times longer to cook than most rices.

Uramaki

Futomaki

Inari

Temaki

Nigiri

Sushi means vinegar rice; sashimi means fish only, no rice.

The literal translation of *su*+*shi* is vinegar+rice. Common forms include:

Nigiri sushi: oblong mounds of vinegar rice topped with a slice of raw or cooked fish, egg, or vegetable, usually with a dab of wasabi between the rice and topping.

Maki sushi: vinegar rice and pieces of fish, egg, and/or vegetables rolled inside or around seaweed (nori), creating a long log that is then cut into bite-sized pieces. Thinner rolls (usually 1 ingredient) are *hosomaki*, thicker ones are *futomaki*, and the inside-out ones are *uramaki*. *Gunkanmaki* is a clump of vinegar rice with a strip of nori around it, creating an edge to contain loose ingredients (fish roe, quail eggs).

65

Temaki: also called a hand roll, it's made the same way as *maki*, but instead of a rolled cylinder, it's tapered into a cone with the ingredients spilling out in the manner of a bouquet. It is eaten by hand, not with chopsticks.

Inari: vinegar rice stuffed into a thin fried tofu pouch.

Less common outside Japan are **bara** (vinegar rice and ingredients mixed as a salad); **chirashi** (layers of fish placed atop a bowl of rice); and **oshizushi** (vinegar rice and ingredients shaped by pressing them into a square mold).

Potatoes can be grown in a bag,
making harvesting easy.

Starch makes the potato.

Potatoes fall into three general categories based on starch and moisture content.

Starchy potatoes are relatively dry and fluffy. They are good for baking, roasting, mashing, and frying. Their ability to absorb liquid makes them an excellent soup thickener. Most varieties are long and have coarse skin. The Russet and Idaho are the most popular; others include the Goldrush and California Long White.

Medium starch potatoes are all-purpose potatoes that are moister than but not as fluffy as starchy potatoes. They hold together well in liquids, and are good for roasting and panfrying. They also can be baked, mashed, or deep-fried. Varieties include Yukon Gold, Yellow Finn, Peruvian Blue, Superior, and Kennebec.

66

Low starch, or waxy, potatoes have a high moisture content and retain their shape when cooked. They are good for potato salads, soups, and other dishes where shape retention is important. Often round with thin smooth skin. Varieties include new, Red Bliss, Round White, and Yellow.

Soft cheeses melt best.

The hardness of cheese is a product of moisture content, compression in the mold, and the length of aging. Soft cheese may contain as much as 80% water, hard grating cheeses only 30%. Soft, high-moisture cheeses melt at around 130°F, hard, low-moisture cheese at 180°F.

Fresh, unripened cheeses (e.g., ricotta, feta) are used in pastries and baking. They are the softest cheeses.

Soft cheeses (brie, camembert) ripen from outside to inside, resulting in a runny center. The longer they are aged, the sharper they taste and smell. They melt very easily.

Semi-soft cheeses (e.g., fontina, port salut) are generally springy to the touch, mild in flavor, and melt easily.

67

Firm or semi-hard cheeses (e.g., cheddar, Swiss, manchego) generally have a strong flavor. They melt somewhat but maintain their shape.

Hard grating cheeses (e.g., romano, parmesan) have the lowest moisture content and become drier when cooked. They will melt only in small shavings.

Put the inexpensive stuff first.

When arranging a buffet, place bread, salads, and similar inexpensive items where diners will encounter them before the main entree and side dishes. This not only matches the order in which most people eat, but discourages them from filling their plates with expensive foods that may end up being wasted.

68

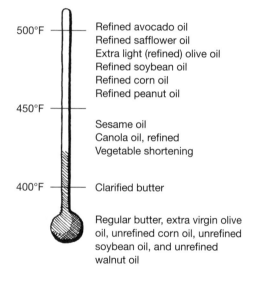

500°F — Refined avocado oil
Refined safflower oil
Extra light (refined) olive oil
Refined soybean oil
Refined corn oil
Refined peanut oil

450°F — Sesame oil
Canola oil, refined
Vegetable shortening

400°F — Clarified butter

Regular butter, extra virgin olive oil, unrefined corn oil, unrefined soybean oil, and unrefined walnut oil

Approximate smoke points

The smoke point

The smoke point is the temperature at which a fat or oil begins to break down and burn, giving food an unpleasant taste and releasing carcinogens into the air and oil. If an oil starts smoking or changing color before food is added, discard the oil and clean the pan.

Beyond the smoke point is the flash point, where combustion occurs.

69

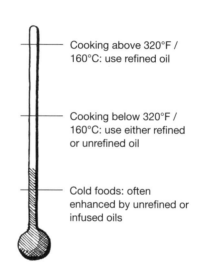

Cooking above 320°F /
160°C: use refined oil

Cooking below 320°F /
160°C: use either refined
or unrefined oil

Cold foods: often
enhanced by unrefined or
infused oils

Refined or unrefined oil?

Unrefined oil is created by directly pressing a food (olives, peanuts, walnuts, etc.). Depending on the specific process and the amount of heat produced, the oil may be labeled "cold pressed," "expeller pressed," or occasionally "expeller cold pressed." Unrefined oils maintain the presence of the original food, and are best used where their greater flavor comes through, such as in salad dressings, sauces, and light cooking (below 320°F).

Refined oils are extracted from foods at high temperatures, often with the use of chemicals. They have a longer shelf life, are clearer and lighter, and have a higher smoke point than unrefined oils, but have fewer nutrients and less flavor. Some have deodorizers, which can cover up processing odors but may prevent one from smelling if the oil has turned rancid. Refined oils are best used for cooking above 320°F, in baking, and in dishes in which the oil does not need to have a flavor.

Infused oils are oils (usually refined) to which a flavor such as garlic, basil, or chili has been added.

Sautéing   Frying   Deep-frying

Proper frying takes place from 350°F to 375°F.

When frying, use an oil with a smoke point above 375°F. Carefully monitor temperature with a thermometer. If too hot, you will burn the food and ruin the oil; too low and the food will take too long to cook and will absorb too much oil. Make sure the food is dry. Cook in small batches, as each item dropped into the oil will lower the temperature. Also keep an eye on food debris in the oil, which can lower the smoke point, and cause burning.

Fire extinguisher types

Class A: paper, wood, cardboard, some plastics.

Class B: combustible liquids including gasoline, kerosene, grease, and oil.

Class C: electrical fires.

Class D: combustible metals.

Class K: recommended for commercial kitchens, as its fine chemical mist prevents grease splash and fire reflash.

How to put out a grease fire

If a fire occurs in a stovetop pan, it usually can be smothered with a pan lid—preferably metal. Salt or baking soda can also be used for smothering, although a lot is required. A rag, blanket, or towel can be used to smother a non-greasy fire, but this should not be the first option.

The best tool is usually a dry chemical fire extinguisher. Blanket the fire with the fine spray mist. Clean up thoroughly afterward, as the chemicals will contaminate the kitchen.

Never pour water on a grease fire, as this will spatter the burning grease and increase the possibility of injury. And never carry a burning vessel to a "safer" place, as this will increase the chances of spreading the fire.

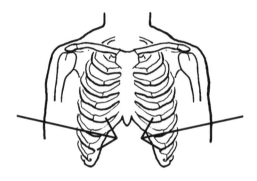

72

Pressure point for the Heimlich maneuver

Quick reactions to emergencies

Cuts: If the cut has ragged edges, tissue or muscle exposed, or if the blood pulses or spurts, call 911. If anything has been severed, wrap in clean plastic wrap, gauze, or cloth and place on ice. There is a 6 to 12 hour window to successfully reattach tissue. Otherwise, press clean cloth to wound, elevate for at least 15 minutes without checking. When bleeding has stopped, gently rinse with water. Ice can reduce swelling.

Burns: Place burn under cool running water for 15 minutes. No ointments, butters, or ice. If the burn blisters, turns white, or is bigger than your hand, call 911. Do not remove any fabric stuck to the burn or break blisters. Cover with a clean bandage, separate burned fingers.

Allergic reactions: Call 911. If the victim carries an EpiPen for allergic reactions, press pen into thigh and hold in place at least 5 seconds. Massage injection site to help absorption. If possible, have person take an antihistamine, lie down with feet elevated, and loosen belts and tight clothing.

73

Choking: Alternate "five and five." With the heel of your hand, hit between the shoulder blades five times. Next, give five abdominal thrusts as you stand behind the person (**Heimlich maneuver**). Repeat until blockage is dislodged.

Call it out!

"Knife!", "Behind you!", "Hot pan!", "Open oven!" must be called out clearly and promptly in a busy kitchen; a polite "excuse me" isn't enough. A failure to communicate effectively can result in someone being burned, cut, or tripped, or dropping what they are carrying.

74

Escherichia coli (E. coli) bacteria

Don't marinate at room temperature.

Marinate foods only in the refrigerator, as colder temperatures retard bacterial growth. Also, never make a sauce out of marinade that was previously used on raw meat, poultry, or seafood, as it will contain bacteria from the uncooked product.

75

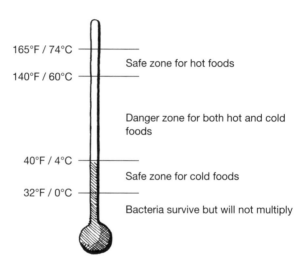

165°F / 74°C — Safe zone for hot foods

140°F / 60°C —

Danger zone for both hot and cold foods

40°F / 4°C — Safe zone for cold foods

32°F / 0°C — Bacteria survive but will not multiply

Cleaning removes dirt. Sanitizing kills germs.

Cleaning is the removal of visible dirt on a surface. **Sanitizing** is the extermination of bacteria and germs by use of steam, hot water (at least 171°F), or a chemical sanitizer.

76

Worcester sauce
anchovies, sardines

Barbecue sauce
pecans

Sweet-and-sour sauce
wheat, soy

Canned tuna
casein, soy protein

Allergens sometimes found in unexpected places

A customer's allergy is a chef's problem.

One in twenty-five people has a food allergy, according to the Food Allergy & Anaphylaxis Network. Peanuts are the leading cause of severe allergic reactions followed by shellfish, fish, tree nuts, and eggs. For some, even a trace amount of an allergen can trigger an extreme reaction.

- Discuss allergy management with staff, and make sure a policy is in place that all are aware of.
- If a dish contains allergens, indicate the specific allergen on the menu, e.g., pecan encrusted trout.
- Don't limit caution to preparation and plating; have the allergen-free dish carried to the table separately from the others.
- Contamination can occur indirectly, via hands/gloves, utensils, pans, even serving trays. If anything—even a garnish—is suspected to have accidentally come in contact with an allergen, make the dish again.

A single pufferfish contains enough poison to kill 30 adults.

Many foods are poisons.

Potatoes: a member of the deadly nightshade family; their leaves and stems as well as the green spots on potato skins contain a glycoalkaloid poison. Death from it is rare, however.

Cherries, plums, apricots, and peaches: contain poisonous compounds in their seeds. Cherry seeds can be crushed to produce a form of cyanide.

Tapioca is from the fruit of the cassava plant, the leaves of which contain cyanide.

Rhubarb: leaves are toxic and house corrosive oxalic acid. The stems and roots are safe.

Bitter almonds contain a form of cyanide in their unprocessed state; a handful can kill an adult. Almonds sold in the U.S. must be heat treated to remove the poison.

Castor beans are so lethal that 4 to 8 can kill an adult. Nonetheless, castor oil is a common health supplement, and is sometimes added to candies, chocolates, and other foods.

Fugu (FOO-goo): a delicacy in Japan and the Philippines, fugu is a pufferfish with a poisonous sac. Approximately 100 people die every year of fugu poisoning.

A $2 chicken can cost $2 million.

Many hazards threaten the safety of staff and customers and the livelihood of a restaurant.

Biological hazards to food come from micro-organisms such as bacteria, molds, yeasts, viruses, fungi, *Staphylococcus aureus*, botulism, *Salmonella*, *Streptococcus*, *E.coli*, and *Listeria*.

Chemical hazards come from cleaning agents, pesticides, and other toxic liquids.

Physical hazards to food are particles such as glass, plastic, metal, wood, dust, and paint chips.

Property hazards include wet, greasy, and slippery floors; icy, poorly lit, or dangerous sidewalks, parking lots, and alleyways; and dangers from buildings, fences, trees, and telephone poles. Restaurants may be liable for the safety of cars, delivery trucks, furniture, kitchen equipment, and customer property inside the restaurant.

Drinking hazards: A 150-pound man typically has a blood alcohol level of .10 after drinking two to four drinks in one hour. Restaurants can be held liable for serving excessive drinks to a customer.

"Everything in moderation, including moderation."

—JULIA CHILD (1912–2004)

80

Peaches, simple biscotti, and other not-too-sweet desserts are excellent complements to most dessert wines.

How to pair wine and food

The richer and fattier the meal, the heavier and fuller the wine should be. Try oak-aged Chardonnay with pasta Alfredo, or Cabernet with steak au poivre.

Spicy and salty meals need fruity, lighter wines. Try Riesling with spicy pork, Rosé with feta cheese, Pinot Grigio with salami.

The more acidic the meal, the more acidic the wine. Sauvignon Blanc with a Greek salad, Zinfandel with ratatouille, Pinot Noir with coq au vin.

When unsure, go with a bridge wine. Pinot Noir is one of the most versatile red wines. Its grapes have high acidity and low tannins, which combine to make it a great pairing for both fish and meats. Chianti and Rioja are also good bridges.

A dessert wine must upstage the dessert in sweetness. If a dessert is sweeter than the dessert wine, the wine's acidity will become more prominent, causing it to taste bitter.

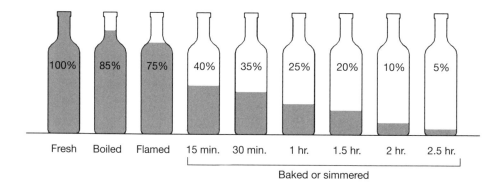

Fresh   Boiled   Flamed   15 min.   30 min.   1 hr.   1.5 hr.   2 hr.   2.5 hr.

Baked or simmered

Percentage of original alcohol remaining after cooking
Source: USDA

Wine substitutes

Sometimes a quick substitution for alcohol is needed because of a customer request or a seldom used liquor is not on hand. The following can be substituted for wine, although it is important to make sure the sweetness level suits the specific dish.

White wine substitutes: white vermouth; chicken stock with white wine vinegar or apple cider vinegar; white grape juice or lemon juice diluted with water; or white wine vinegar with the juice from canned mushrooms.

Red wine substitutes: red vermouth; beef stock with red wine vinegar or apple cider vinegar; red grape juice diluted with water; red wine vinegar; or a small amount of tomato paste with the juice from canned mushrooms.

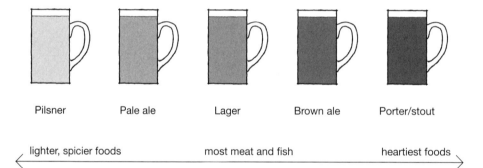

Pilsner   Pale ale   Lager   Brown ale   Porter/stout

lighter, spicier foods   most meat and fish   heartiest foods

Don't hesitate to recommend a beer pairing.

Beer is the world's oldest and most popular alcoholic beverage, and the third most consumed beverage after water and tea. Almost everyone has a favorite beer, but not every beer works well with every food. Consider having recommended beer pairings as well as wine pairings on your menu. Lighter beers generally go with light dishes, darker beer with heartier meals. A hoppy beer can intensify the experience of a spicy dish, and can cut through a fattier meal.

83

Fresh name

Jalapeno

Chilaca

Pimiento or Tomato

Mirasol

Poblano (chili)

Dry name

Chipotle (smoked)

Pasilla

Paprika

Guajillo

Ancho (ripened first) /
    Mulato (not ripened)

Red pepper, the most widely consumed spice in the world, often
changes names when going from fresh to dried.

Drying intensifies flavor.

Fresh herbs may be 80% or more water. When dried, most become two to three times more potent, although they lose flavor over time. Oregano, sage, rosemary, and thyme tend to retain the most flavor when dried, and work best in long-cooking dishes. Delicate herbs such as basil, chives, tarragon, and dill lose flavor when dried and are best used in fresh form and added at the end of cooking.

Toasting spices right before grinding or cooking further intensifies flavor.

84

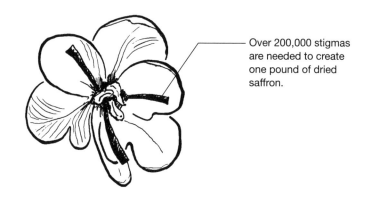

Over 200,000 stigmas are needed to create one pound of dried saffron.

Saffron flower

Spices were once used as money.

Spices were used for trade or barter in many early civilizations, including the Fertile Crescent and Rome. In the Roman empire, workers were often paid in salt, hence the word "salary." When the Visigoths attacked Rome in 408 CE, they demanded 3,000 pounds of pepper as part of the city's ransom. In 14th century Europe, saffron counterfeiters became such a problem that the *Safranschou* code was enacted, under which saffron defrauders were thrown in prison and even executed. Genuine saffron today can cost over $1,000 per pound at retail.

Day of the year on which eggs were graded and packed (e.g., 181st day of the year). Usually dated within a week of being laid, although it could be up to 30 days later.

Sell-by date: not required by U.S. law, but if the USDA shield is used, must be within 45 days of the pack date. The USDA states that eggs are good for consumption for three to five weeks after the sell-by date. When confused by dates, use the day of the year to best gauge freshness.

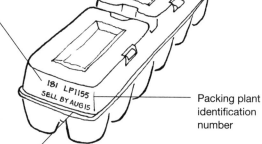

181 LP1155
SELL BY AUG 15

Packing plant identification number

Egg dating

The fresher the egg, the more flavorful and colorful the yolk and the better the white will hold its shape. In savory cooking, the texture and flavor of eggs is often most important, while in baking their structural properties can become particularly significant as they help bind other ingredients. Freshness also helps promote greater volume in baked products, and guards against dangers in desserts such as crème anglaise, buttercreams, and mousses, in which eggs might not be heated enough to kill bacteria.

Hunter/gatherers liked flatbreads.

Crude forms of flatbread were first found around 10,000 BCE. By 3,000 BCE Egyptians were making leavened yeast-raised breads. Ancient flatbreads were made by mixing wild wheats such as einkorn and emmer with water, and baking the mixture in a brick or clay oven heated as high as 480°F.

Flatbreads today use a similar recipe of flour/grain mixed with water and salt. They include the tortilla (Mexico), injera (Ethiopia), naan (India), and matzoh (Israel).

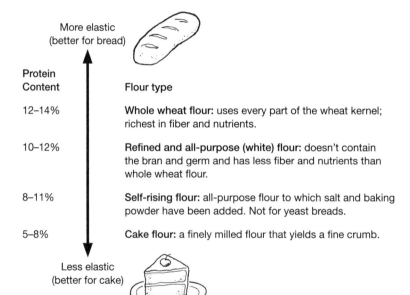

More elastic
(better for bread)

Protein Content

Flour type	
12–14%	**Whole wheat flour:** uses every part of the wheat kernel; richest in fiber and nutrients.
10–12%	**Refined and all-purpose (white) flour:** doesn't contain the bran and germ and has less fiber and nutrients than whole wheat flour.
8–11%	**Self-rising flour:** all-purpose flour to which salt and baking powder have been added. Not for yeast breads.
5–8%	**Cake flour:** a finely milled flour that yields a fine crumb.

Less elastic
(better for cake)

Select flour by protein content.

Protein content in wheat flour determines the amount of gluten and resulting elasticity. Bread dough needs the elastic gluten strands to trap yeast gasses, which give bread its desired chewiness and air pockets. In cakes, a lower gluten flour is needed for a finer, lighter crumb and minimal chewiness. Hard red wheat produces flour that is high in protein and gluten, while soft red wheat yields lower gluten flours.

Semolina flour (from durum wheat) is the exception to the protein-gluten rule, as it's high in protein but its gluten is not as elastic, making it perfect for pasta and couscous.

1 cup
unsifted
flour

1 cup
sifted
flour

1 cup
flour,
sifted

4.94 oz. ±

3.95 oz.±

3.95 oz.

Sifted flour is not the same as flour, sifted.

Baking is often said to be a science; slight inaccuracies in measurement can cause dramatic failure. The wrong flour or too much of the right flour can produce a tough, dry product; too little may cause a collapse.

To measure flour accurately, don't dip a measuring cup directly into the flour, as it will compact and you may end up with 20% more flour than intended. Instead, use a measuring cup that is exactly one cup to the brim. Fill it to overflowing with a scoop or spoon, and then gently level it off with a knife. However, even this method can produce results that vary by an ounce or more.

Weighing is the most accurate method of measuring flour.

Freeze for ease.

Cookies: for thick cookies, put dough in the freezer for 30 minutes before baking. This will keep the fat from melting before the other ingredients, and will produce a deliciously thick cookie instead of a flat-all-over cookie.

Pastry dough: warmer butter can blend too much with flour, resulting in dense dough. Freezing butter pieces for 20 to 30 minutes before adding them to flour will keep them cold and separate, resulting in buttery pockets that produce a flakey crust.

Raw beef is easier to slice thinly, as often called for in stir-fry dishes, if placed in the freezer for 30 to 60 minutes. **Bacon** is likewise easier to slice if put in a freezer for 15 to 20 minutes.

Oysters and other shellfish are easier to open when chilled; 10 to 15 minutes in a freezer will relax the seal.

90

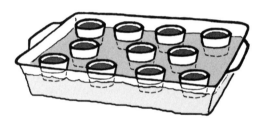

Water your oven!

When baking cheesecakes, custards, puddings, and other fragile egg dishes, place the pan in a water bath to promote even cooking and prevent curdling. The oven temperature may fluctuate, but the *bain marie* will stay at a steady 212°F.

When baking French baguettes or boules (country loaves), place a broiler pan in the oven while preheating, beneath the bread pan or baking stone. Pour a cup of water into the pan just before putting the bread in the oven. The steam will attract sugars in the bread to the surface, where they will caramelize and produce a crisp crust.

Sweetbreads have nothing to do with bread.

Animal parts that are unappetizing to many palates are often served as delicacies around the world. Sweetbreads come from the thymus or pancreas glands of beef, lamb, and pork. They are commonly prepared by first brining and then soaking in milk. They are then grilled, breaded and fried, stuffed, or used in stuffings and pâtés.

Head cheese is made from the head, ears, tongue, heart, and sometimes feet of a pig, calf, cow, or sheep. The parts are boiled until the meat falls off the bone. The meat and juices are then put into a pan or other mold. As the product cools, its natural aspic solidifies. It is served cold and sliced.

Goats discovered coffee.

Ever since meat first fell into the fire or milk churned into butter or separated into cheese during a rough journey, foods have been discovered and created in unusual, accidental ways.

Coffee was first consumed by humans in the 9th century, after an Ethiopian goat herder noticed his goats becoming agitated from eating coffee berries.

Roquefort cheese arose when a shepherd left his bread and cheese in a cave to pursue a lass in the next field. When he returned a few weeks later, he discovered the bread mold had shot through the cheese, creating the now-famous taste.

Potato chips are alleged to have been created after a customer sent back fried potatoes, complaining they were thick and soggy. The bitter chef sliced them as thin as possible and fried them so hard they couldn't be eaten with a fork.

Saccharin was discovered when a researcher forgot to wash his hands of chemicals, and found his bread was sweeter where he had held it.

Ice cream cones are said to have first appeared at the 1904 World's Fair when an ice cream vendor ran out of serving bowls. A helpful pastry maker made cones of pastry to hold the ice cream, and the result was a smash hit.

93

How to survive when lost in the kitchen

Learn the menu immediately. This will improve your timing when it's busy.

Prepare. Show up early, walk around, learn where everything is, and take notes on how things are done. Ask other workers the particulars of each piece of equipment.

Learn the culture of the kitchen. See if it is quiet or happy-go-lucky, and fit in.

Don't stand around. When not busy, see if anyone, including the dishwasher, needs help.

Constantly check your station and scan your area during slow periods to make sure everything is in place and every container is full. You will not have time to go to the walk-in refrigerator or freezer when the kitchen gets busy. When orders arrive, scan again to verify that you have everything needed to prepare them.

Concentrate. Keep talking to a minimum and focus on the orders. Repeat everything the expeditor says *to* the expeditor and say it twice more in your head.

94

Breathe. A kitchen's busy period can provide an exhilarating "rush," but when things are hectic take an occasional brief moment to reflect on what is happening.

"Success seems to be connected with action. Successful people keep moving. They make mistakes, but they don't quit."

—CONRAD HILTON, hotel executive

95

Why the chef's jacket is double breasted

The front of a chef's jacket is reversible. This allows a chef to wear the clean side over the dirty side if entering the dining room to greet guests.

Additionally, the double layer of heavy cotton protects against hot spills and splatters. Cloth toggles are used instead of buttons, which can snag, break, or melt into food. The vented cuffs turn up, getting them out of the way of foods and leaving a fresh edge to turn down when entering the dining room.

Surprising items in a chef's toolkit

Dental floss: for cutting layer cakes, roll cookies, soft cheeses, dough, and cheesecake.

Nail polish or plasticized paint: for putting identifying marks on one's tools.

Tweezers or needle nosed pliers: for removing pin bones from fish and fragments of eggshell.

Small spray bottles: for moistening pie dough, coating pans with oil, and misting salad dressing on delicate greens.

Bricks: cleaned and wrapped in foil, used in preparing dishes such as pollo al mattone, an Italian recipe in which chicken is cooked under a weight, producing crisp skin and juicy meat in about half the normal cooking time.

Ruler: for measuring the amount of rise in dough, the size or thickness of steaks and other foods, and for leveling the contents of measuring cups.

Take it to the cooler.

If a disagreement arises, you need to blow off steam, the kitchen is too hot, or a private conversation with a coworker is called for, have someone cover your station for a few minutes and—assuming it won't suggest impropriety—use the walk-in cooler. It's nearly soundproof, and the cold will help you resolve your problem quickly.

A cook knows how to make something; a chef knows why to make it that way.

All chefs are cooks, but not all cooks are chefs. A cook does the everyday *mise en place* for a station or the entire kitchen but may only work on one station. A chef oversees all the cooks and knows how to expertly work all stations. Cooks are usually paid hourly and receive overtime pay, while a chef is salaried and is not paid overtime. A cook may prepare a dish that is delivered to the dining room, but the chef's name and reputation are attached to it.

Most significantly, a cook cooks from the head and is more likely to follow a recipe. A chef cooks from the head *and* the heart, and knows that an understanding of ingredients and technique trumps any recipe.

99

A chef's routine is the customer's special event.

The repetition of a chef's job can be wearying as the same dishes are prepared and served again and again. But for a customer, a request for a dish may be the only time he or she ever has that meal. The twelfth rack of lamb you've prepared in a night is the first you've prepared for that customer. The ordinary to you may be the extraordinary to a guest.

The Culinarian's Code

I pledge my professional knowledge and skill
to the advancement of our profession and to

I shall be too big for worry, too noble for
anger, too strong for fear, and too happy to
permit the pressure of business to hurt anyone,
within or without the profession.

by American Culinary Federation, 1957

"Anybody can make you enjoy the first bite of a dish, but only a real chef can make you enjoy the last."

—FRANÇOIS MINOT,
French chef and restaurant consultant (1936–)

Louis Eguaras is a culinary professor at the California School of Culinary Arts, Le Cordon Bleu Program. A former White House chef, he has cooked for foreign dignataries and celebrities including Nelson Mandela, Tom Hanks, Jimmy Buffett, Anthony Hopkins, Oliver Stone, James Woods, Mick Jagger and the Rolling Stones, and Crosby, Stills, and Nash. He lives in Valencia, California.

Matthew Frederick is an architect, urban designer, teacher, author of the bestselling *101 Things I Learned in Architecture School*, and the creator, editor, and illustrator of the 101 Things I Learned series. He lives in Cambridge, Massachusetts.